*How To Mal*

# Make Money Online

## 50 Ways To Make Money From Home Including Selling Niche Website Portfolios, Ebay, Fiverr, Blogging, Passive Income Strategies And More!

**James Harper**

Copyright © 2015 James Harper

# STOP!!! Before you read any further….Would you like to know the Success Secrets of how to make Passive Income Online?

If your answer is yes, then you are not alone. Thousands of people are looking for the secret to learning how to create their own online passive income style business.

If you have been searching for these answers without much luck, you are in the right place!

Because I want to make sure to give you as much value as possible for purchasing this book, right now for a limited time you can get 3 incredible bonuses for free.

At the end of this book I describe all 3 bonuses. You can access them at the end. But for those of you that want to grab your bonuses right now. See below.

<u>Just Go Here For Free Instant Access:</u>

www.OperationAwesomeLife.com/FreeBonuses

## Legal Notice

All rights reserved. Without limiting the rights under the copyright reserved above, no part of this publication may be reproduced, stored in or introduced into a retrieval system, or transmitted, in any form, or by any means (electronic, mechanical, photocopying, recording, or otherwise) without the prior written permission of the copyright owner and publisher of this book. This book is copyright protected. This is for your personal use only. You cannot amend, distribute, sell, use, quote or paraphrase any part or the content within this eBook without the consent of the author or copyright owner. Legal action will be pursued if this is breached.

## Disclaimer Notice

Please note the information contained within this document is for educational and entertainment purposes only. Considerable energy and every attempt has been made to provide the most up to date, accurate, relative, reliable, and complete information, but the reader is strongly encouraged to seek professional advice prior to using any of this information contained in this book. The reader understands they are reading and using this information contained herein at their own risk, and in no way will the author, publisher, or any affiliates be held responsible for any damages whatsoever. No warranties of any kind are expressed or implied. Readers acknowledge that the author is not engaging in the rendering of legal, financial, medical, or any other professional advice. By reading this document, the reader agrees that under no circumstances is the author, publisher, or anyone else affiliated with the production, distribution, sale, or any other element of this book responsible for any losses, direct or indirect, which are incurred as a result of the use of information contained within this document, including, but not limited to, -errors, omissions, or inaccuracies. Because of the rate with which conditions change, the author and publisher reserve the right to alter and update the information contained herein on the new conditions whenever they see applicable.

# Table Of Contents

Introduction

Chapter 1: 50 Top Ways To Make Money From Home

Chapter 2: 4 Best Ways Of Making Money Online For Beginners

Chapter 3: 15 Ways To Make Money By Blogging

Chapter 4: 3 Ways To Make Money By Facebook Marketing

Chapter 5: 3 Ways To Make Money Through Affiliate Marketing

Chapter 6: 4 Ways To Make Money Through Fiverr

Chapter 7: 3 Ways To Make Money By Drop Shipping

Chapter 8: 4 Ways To Make Money Through eBay

Chapter 9: 3 Ways To Make Money By Selling Niche Website Portfolios

Chapter 10: 5 Ways To Make Money Through Different Passive Income Strategies

Conclusion

Preview Of: "Hot Small Business Ideas! 25 Smokin' Hot Start Up Business Ideas To Spark Your Entrepreneurship Creativity And Have You In Business Fast!"

Check Out My Other Books

Free Bonus Offer

# Introduction

I want to thank you and congratulate you for purchasing the book, *"Make Money Online: How To Make Money Online! - 50 Ways To Make Money From Home Including Selling Niche Website Portfolios, eBay, Fiverr, Blogging, Passive Income Strategies And More!"*

This "Make Money Online" book contains proven steps and strategies on how to start earning through the web without the intricacies and capitals involved in setting up a real business. You can choose from any of the 50 ways listed here, depending on your interests.

After you have picked a particular income-generating activity, you need to study it carefully and dedicate time and energy for it to succeed. The failure rate here is relatively low, so you can experiment or just push further according to your desire.

Thanks again for purchasing this book, I hope you enjoy it!

# Chapter 1: 50 Top Ways To Make Money From Home

As this book introduces you to the top 50 ways to make money from the comforts of your home, it is best to start the list with the six most promising long-term careers online that you can try.

## 1. Template Sales

Did you know that designing website themes and templates can earn you $20 to $200 per sale? It is a growing trend that has also been proven lucrative. As more people now want to have their own website, the demand for unique templates also increases. What's great about it is that it is considered a hybrid of graphic designing and blogging, which means you, can venture in it even with average technical knowledge as long as you have unfathomable artistry.

Although usually meant for custom-orders, it can also have the potential to give you passive income. Check out DIY Themes and StudioPress to learn more about the business.

## 2. Travel Management

Scouting for places to spend a vacation and booking for reservations and transportation tickets are now easier, thanks to the internet. However, it does not change the fact that arranging for so many things before a well-planned vacation takes time – lots of it – making it inconvenient for many people, such as professionals and retirees.

As a travel manager, your job is to search for and present possible destinations to your clients. Once approved, you take care of all the inclusive arrangements, from booking and reservation to hiring tour guides and car rentals.

## 3. Outsourcing Management

Many website owners and businesses need a lot of different services for short- or long-term projects. In fact, there are so many that they no longer have the time to hire, interview, and manage the projects alongside their main ventures. An outsourcing manager helps in making sure that all services are provided according to standards and contracts, all deadlines are met, and all liaison matters are taken care of.

An outsourcing manager either earns per contract, per project, per number of services or freelancers managed, or per output. Also throw in a couple of bonuses and you're good.

## 4. HR Management

Freelancers are all over the internet. There are a lot of candidates that make the selection process harder for virtual employers. This is where your service as an HR associate enters the picture. The potential for this online venture to earn you big income is huge because e-lancing is a growing niche and potential clients and applicants never come short.

Many clients would also hire HR associates to do the screening process, hiring, and training for all applicants selected from freelancing marketplaces, such as oDesk, Elance, Fiverr, Guru, and TaskRabbit, among others.

## 5. Email Management

An email manager partly fulfills the job of a virtual assistant. However, his primary responsibility is to manage the marketing list and generate some more through follow-ups and correspondence. Usually, he is also in charge in the creation of newsletters and other printable marketing materials, such as catalogues and banner ads.

This is a specialty niche that deals with email marketers and networkers. Thus, you have a concentrated clientele, making the job even more in demand.

## 6. E-learning Development

Online education and training from kids to professionals are part of a growing industry that requires interactive learning modules and innovative methods of teaching. Unfortunately, this new industry is still lacking e-learning developers since many choose to just venture on tutorial services without thinking of the appropriate learning materials first. Unlike eBook writers, e-learning developers work on a variety of mediums that can be tapped for pedagogical purposes.

# Chapter 2: 4 Best Ways Of Making Money Online For Beginners

For novices who are still in the process of discovering the internet's huge potential in creating your own business, here are four basic ways to make money online.

### *7. Pay Per Click (PPC)*

PPC is considered the most basic blog monetization option today. You just have to set-up your blog, start writing, and register it with an advertising program of your choice. It is synonymous to online advertising, although the concept is actually broad and may pertain to other types of income-generating activities.

The mechanics here is that you place ads (which you can choose, depending on your set-up) on your blog, and then you earn with varying rate for every click your visitors make. A simple click is normally worth a few cents, while a click with successful transaction (e.g. registration) is worth more.

Must try PPC programs include Google Adsense, AdBrite, Bidvetiser, and Chitika.

### *8. Editing*

You do not need a degree to offer editing service, unless you are targeting academic writers and researchers. All you need here is good grammar and creative instinct. Many professional bloggers have ideas but just do not have the linguistic ability to uphold quality output for international readers. Many eBook writers also need editorial guidance to make their works sellable. Even businessmen, speakers, and coaches now hire editors to make sure that their speeches and lectures are effective and affective.

Currently, there are over a million eBooks sold in Amazon, and that is just a portion of the market you can play on.

## 9. Paid Surveys

You won't find financial success in this career, but it is a decent sideline if you are looking for extra cash and some freebies. You guessed it right; you just have to answer online surveys and get paid for it. However, there are many surveys that are looking for a specific demographic, so you have to find the right fit.

For instances when monetary payment is not an option, the client (the one who paid for the survey) sends out products to try, or electronic vouchers. They can be as simple as a new energy drink or a high-end appliance. Either way, you get to collect free samples (and perhaps sell them afterwards).

## 10. SEO Writing

SEO writers are some of the most in-demand professionals. They just do not run out of potential clients. They write web contents, blog posts, newsletter, or practically anything that needs search engine optimization for higher ranking and improved online visibility. You can earn anywhere from $35,000 to $80,000 a year just by being a fulltime SEO writer – not exactly a hard thing to do if you love writing.

# Chapter 3: 15 Ways To Make Money By Blogging

For bloggers who want to take their hobby to the next level and become a fulltime professional blogger, here are 15 ways to do it.

### *11. Cost Per Thousand (CPM)*

The "M" is "1000" in roman numerals, just in case you are wondering. You also have to join an advertising program like in PPC, only you are paid for the impression and not for the clicks. It means that your earn depending on the times the ads are seen by visitors. Naturally, the more traffic you get, the bigger your income will be.

As the name implies, CPM programs usually pay for every thousand views. The price also varies although it depends on the niche you are in and the amount of traffic you get.

The best CPM programs to try are Tribal Fusion and Value Click.

### *12. Money Widget*

This is an alternative for bloggers who like to put online ads but want less invasiveness. Compared to PPC and CPM where ads pop up on various places within your page – places that you select – a money widget typically shows ads only on the sidebar or wherever you place the widget. It means that your page will remain clean, and you will have full control over the appearance of ads. It does not make much money like other advertising programs do, but it is more organized and looks more professional.

You may want to check out SmartLinks and WidgetBucks.

### *13. Sponsorship*

Also called private ad sales, it is a way of blogging for your sponsors who pay you either for the impression, successful referral, or click. Fashion blogger BryanBoy is being paid this way, albeit usually, in kind (as in luxury bags and accessories!). There are bloggers who also use in-text ads to serve as their referral/affiliate link. You've been seeing these as hyperlinks within blog posts.

When you accept a sponsorship, you practically become an informal publicist. It should not really bother you if you have really good and credible sponsors. However, you might be compromising your blog's quality and credibility if you will promote "shady" ones.

## *14. Donations*

Wikipedia has been surviving on donations; yet, it continues to grow indefinitely. The idea might sound lame from a business standpoint, but it actually works if you have something valuable to offer. It practically applies the concept of reward: you give unique and helpful information and your readers provide you with donations...hopefully. There is no guarantee to it, but it works most of the time. Just be great in what you do. Make your blog indispensable until your readers start to rely on you.

## *15. Feed Ads*

It is essentially the same with PPC and CPM, only the ads are placed on your feeds instead of your webpages. This is a good strategy if you have a long mailing list waiting for your feeds everyday but want to maintain a clean and professional-looking website free of promotions.

You just have to register for an RSS feed, and then monetize it with Google Adsense. You approach a targeted market this way, so that also means higher fee.

## *16. Premium Content/Membership*

How do you think membership porn sites flourish? Before you raise an eyebrow, understand first that many porn sites employ some of the most lucrative strategies (*Alexa*lists a couple of porn sites in the top 50 most-visited websites in the world). They share free contents but leave visitors wanting more, enough to force them to sign up for the premium contents.

You do not have to join the porn industry because it is applicable to all niches. In fact, SEOMoz, a top SEO-instructional website, has been earning from this strategy for years now. Membership sites also create a community of targeted market where you can source your data from. That in itself is already a commodity waiting to be sold.

## 17. Paid Reviews

As opposed to sponsorship, it is a more direct approach albeit with little or no bias involved. A paid reviewer is normally paid to write a straight review, sometimes with the inclusion of an affiliate link. What the client wants here is the exposure your traffic can provide. Besides, a good product does not need a biased review to sell.

It can be a regular gig if you own a review blog in a particular niche.

## 18. Continuity Programs

This is an umbrella term referring to various services offered by websites, such as premium membership, newsletters, eBooks, webinars, and virtual consultations, among others. Contrary to membership-based websites, those with continuity programs give actual free services. Some offer free coaching while others free book editing – anything to keep visitors signed in and paying.

Websites can earn thousands every month from this strategy alone. It does not matter if you are merely running a blog or an entire company. For as long as you can offer different valuable services all at the same time, it should work for you.

## 19. Job Boards

What started as a Craigslist spinoff turned out to be a lucrative online venture. Take a look at oDesk's and Elance's combined eight million freelancers and two-million-business clientele. Don't they sound like money to you?

There is an on-going trend of adding job boards in frequented blogs because the traffic is also high yet the cost for clients is lower. Compared to major e-lancing marketplaces, blog job boards normally charge for every post and not for the services rendered. For instance, instead of paying 10% to 25% of the total service rendered to the big e-lancing sites, a client will only have to pay a one-time fee for the post regardless of the amount of service rendered.

### 20. Event Sponsorship

Once you've established your traffic, you can hold big events and get sponsors for them. Many bloggers do it in the form of "blogathons" (also a good way to attract guest bloggers), contests, or webinars. To make the event more attractive, you can throw in some cash and giveaways, of course. Don't worry, you can get the cost back from your sponsors, in addition to the long-term benefit of the increased traffic.

Some people think that sponsorship is somehow difficult. However, it is practically the same with getting advertisers, so it should not be a problem especially if you have a high traffic to boast.

### 21. Page Rental

This concept is somehow new but has since seen in practice with the prevalence of professional blogging. It entails having one main page in your blog rented out to a third party, mostly for e-commerce and press release purposes.

For instance, if you are in the health niche and currently enjoying high traffic, a supplement manufacturer or distributor might want to rent your page for its press releases. Or, if you run a review site, a product distributor might want to rent your page for online shopping. The idea is more practical for clients because the traffic and website are already there.

## 22. Blogging Network

Essentially, it is the same with blog sponsorship, only this time, you will be working alongside other bloggers (thus, the network) to achieve a common goal under a large brand. For instance, a certain company is launching a new product and it needs to employ online marketing to create a buzz. It will hire an entire network of bloggers that will be talking about the same thing with different approaches and different styles. This is to make the buzz look more authentic.

It will open big opportunity for you because you will not only be able to earn from the client but also establish connection with other bloggers with the same interest, and use the network for your own marketing campaign.

## 23. E-commerce

If you have many visitors, you also have many potential buyers. That makes an e-commerce/online shopping site a really promising online business for you. You can go by simply promoting products and allowing orders directly from your site, or by integrating online catalogue to your pages with one-click order buttons for convenience.

It is up to you to sell your own products or consign for other manufacturers or distributors. If you do not have a website, try doing it first using social media sites, such as Instagram and Facebook.

Also check out CafePress and Printfection to learn more about starting an online shop.

## 24. Coaching

As you share your expertise on your blog, you can take it to a new level by offering personal coaching services. Coaching is a major contributor in the income of many marketing specialists, and it can be your biggest source of income too. You can guide clients through daily consultations, newsletters, emails and webinars.

Nonetheless, you need to get certifications and memberships if you really want to build credibility in a certain field. You need to be someone to look up to, and that can only happen if you have something to brag about.

## 25. *Webinars*

Web seminar is a growing trend because it is more convenient for coaches and clients. The best thing about it is that you can get unlimited audience anywhere in the world, which means unlimited income for you. There are live and canned webinars, but focus groups want live interactions, so that they can exchange ideas and ask questions as well. There is no standard pricing for webinars, but the more unique and extensive your topic is, the higher you can demand.

# Chapter 4: 3 Ways To Make Money By Facebook Marketing

If you want to turn your pastime into a lucrative form of home business, Facebook is the best social media platform you can use. Here are three ways to make money from it.

### 26. Social Media Manager

As more personalities, such as celebrities and businessmen, use the social media to preserve visibility and maintain interaction with followers or clients, the demand for social media managers also increase, specifically for public relations management and customer service purposes. Do you really think that busy personalities juggle social media interactions and their busy schedules all by themselves? Social media managers ensure that information make it across both sides while ensuring that the profiles are presentable and engaging all at the same time. This is a pretty lucrative job yet easy to do especially for people who have nothing to do but spend time on Facebook and other sites.

### 27. Social Media Marketer

With the specific task of marketing products and services, contents, or updates, a social media marketer plays an essential role towards the completion of many internet marketing plans. The social media is a whole new platform comprised of different websites and communicative tools. It needs a dedicated professional for the strategy to become successful. If you have extensive knowledge in the social media and have background in marketing, this can be the new venture for you. A bonus: you practically have unlimited clientele.

### 28. Facebook Marketing Manager

It is essentially the same with a social media manager, only this time, you will also be given e-commerce responsibilities. Facebook is now often used for business transactions because it has all the capabilities a businessman needs to sell – videos, pictures, and message boards. Your job is not only to manage contents and communication, but also the presentation of products down to the selling.

# Chapter 5: 3 Ways To Make Money Through Affiliate Marketing

If you are into affiliate marketing, do not waste your time promoting products from vendors that do not pay. Here are the three biggest and best affiliate programs you can try.

### *29. Amazon Associates*

Amazon's own is the biggest affiliate marketing program across all industries to date. As a matter of fact, with over 900,000 associates under their belt, they have marketing presence in at least 1.2% of all websites on the planet.

Making money through this affiliate program is easy. You just need to have a website, like a blog, promote one of Amazon's millions of products, and lead your visitors to the sales page via an affiliate link. You get advertising fees (essentially commissions) for every successful purchase, with the rate varying according to the category of the product, from 1% for video game console products to 10% for Amazon coins and jewelry products.

Amazon is the biggest online shopping site today, so you should not have any problem making a sale.

### *30. CJ Affiliate*

If Amazon Associate is the biggest worldwide, CJ Affiliate (formerly Commission Junction) is the biggest in the US with strong presence in the top 1,000 online retailers. The Cost Per Action (CPA) system of this affiliate program is more likely to earn users than any other program today. In fact, their top 500 earners tend to earn more than that of Amazon. The only difference is that CJ Affiliate has full program management with recruitment and optimization support options.

### *31. ClickBank*

It was the biggest affiliate network in the US last 2011, but even if a huge number of its 1,500,000 affiliate marketers are no longer active, it is still one of the most viable and lucrative income-generating activities online. ClickBank has more than 46,000 products to promote, so you will never run out of options come marketing time.

# Chapter 6: 4 Ways To Make Money Through Fiverr

Fiverr is one of the fastest-rising online marketplaces for people who have a service to offer. Price usually starts at $5. Now decide which services you can give for five dollars.

### *32. Newsletter Writing*

Have you ever noticed that a lot of blogs start to offer newsletters lately? This is a strategy to maintain traffic and at the same time, generate marketing leads and successfully perform email marketing. However, a lot of bloggers, especially those that also offer other services like coaching, do not really have the time to write all the materials and manage the website at the same time. Thus, newsletter writing is often outsourced.

What's interesting with this venture is that you can secure clients even by directly contacting bloggers or posting on job boards.

### *33. Virtual assistance*

Many employers, especially those into online businesses, now prefer virtual assistants because they are dependable anytime yet more affordable. They do not require benefits but still have the same range of services actual office assistants offer. If you have experience in office administration, data management, and secretarial work, this is a great way to make money without leaving your home.

Although the basic pay in Fiverr starts at $5.00 per hour, you can go higher depending on the services you will offer. You can demand a little extra for writing and designing services, what have you.

### *34. Translation*

It is almost like all online businessmen want syndication to cover bigger market, thereby improving their chances of earning. This includes but not limited to web contents, eBooks, social media pages, newsletters, and email correspondence. If you are multilingual, being a translator will certainly pay off big time since this service demands premium. The European market in particular shows the biggest potential as more publishers here want to reach the American market for the similarity in information needs.

### 35. Graphic Designing

Who does not need graphic designing nowadays? Websites, books, and newsletters – this service is essential. Even in the age of do-it-yourself collages and templates, graphic designing still remains one of the most in-demand online services, and one proof to that is the prevalence of job posts – or sold service for that matter – on Fiverr.

What makes this venture very promising is the fact that no matter how convenient it is to make personalized graphic designs, many clients will still not have time to do it; thus, they pay you for your service and your time.

# Chapter 7: 3 Ways To Make Money By Drop Shipping

Drop shipping is the practice of selling and marketing products that are not in your possession but are available for delivery straight from the manufacturer. It allows you to earn interest by applying your marketing expertise.

### *36. Private Label Drop Shipping*

When you have so many ideas for a type of product but do not have the capital to fund the manufacturing process, you can resort to private label drop shipping or the practice of having customized products made for you but only to be delivered upon order. This system requires extensive feasibility study to make sure that you are targeting the right market and you have solid marketing plan.

### *37. Online Cataloguing*

It is the practice of marketing different sets of products in the form of online catalogues but without actual stocks involved. This is the perfect online business if you have the knack for internet marketing and want to earn from purchases without physical products. The net income depends on your interest, which can reach more than double the price from the manufacturer.

### *38. Online Auction*

This is the principle behind eBay's product auctions. Listing a product in the website does not necessarily mean you have it. What you have is the guarantee that it can be delivered to the bidder at the right time. You can also create your own website for online auction purposes.

# Chapter 8: 4 Ways To Make Money Through eBay

eBay is more than a selling and auction site. It offers other income opportunities that you can do even without products to sell.

### *39. Selling*

It is basically what eBay is for. You can sell anything for as long as they are not included in the company's prohibited items, such as alcohol, tobacco, drugs, and firearms, among others. You also have the choice to list your merchandize under an online auction.

eBay is also giving incentives to their Power Sellers which belong to five levels according to the monthly income: bronze, silver, gold, platinum, and titanium.

### *40. eBay Online Affiliate Program*

eBay's own affiliate program allows referrers to earn $2.00 for every seller they can recruit plus 5% for of what their referrals will earn through the same program. In a way, it is a type of passive income that allows you to earn even when you are no longer actively recruiting. Imagine how much you can earn if you can refer 10 people in one day and those 10 people also recruit the same number on a daily basis within a whole month. For a day's effort, you can earn $900 without doing anything.

You can get the referral links from Commission Junction.

### *41. eBay Selling Instructor Program*

If you have success in selling and want to share your secrets, eBay's Selling Instructor Program is the right income-generating activity for you. All you have to do is apply, get trained, teach on your free time, and receive incentives. Your earnings will be determined by how much your students will also earn within a year. And because all of their listed items will fall under your own incentive program, you can incur passive income for as long as they continue selling in the website.

## 42. eBay Trading Assistant Affiliate Program

The website has a lot of member sellers but not all of them know how to market their products properly. This is where you offer your help. You assist on other sellers' marketing strategies and receive incentive for every successful sale. You will also be entitled to a $300 bonus if you will reach a certain threshold.

To be a trading assistant, you have to apply and undergo training as well. However, you can just wait for direct invitation from eBay if you are already a selling instructor.

# Chapter 9: 3 Ways To Make Money By Selling Niche Website Portfolios

Here are three ways to make money by selling niche website portfolios.

### 43. Selling of domains

It is not exactly called selling portfolios. Rather, it is selling the website itself. You will be investing on the domain name instead of the content, so you need less time and capital yet the return is potentially huge.

How to make an empty website sellable? You have to proactively buy a domain before it is wanted by other parties. Foresightedness is essential.

For instance, if you think that a certain name, term, catchphrase, or anything buzz-worthy is apt to be huge in the future, register a domain name after it and just wait for the right time when it becomes valuable.

### 44. Selling of Private Forums

A growing online community can be your own expensive commodity. All you have to do is start a private online forum site with targeted market to create a network of contacts. It will serve as a discussion and virtual socialization place for people with similar interests. Once the community grows, you can discreetly sell it to a third party that is willing to pay for all the sure leads and information he can get. From a buyer's angle, it is like selling marketing leads, survey answers, and market research all in one.

### 45. Site Flipping

This is the practice of buying a dormant website and improving it in terms of design, content, and traffic to make it more marketable – basically the same principle behind house flipping. Why do you have to buy an existing website instead of creating a new one? It is for the domain name. It also helps if the website has had a decent traffic in the past but the owner decided to discontinue the management for some reason.

This usually requires an extensive work, so you might want to look at outsourcing to get the flipping done faster (especially helpful if you are flipping numerous sites at the same time)

.

# Chapter 10: 5 Ways To Make Money Through Different Passive Income Strategies

Passive income means continuous earnings without actively doing anything else other than the initial effort. Here are five ways to earn passively minus the hard work.

### 46. Parked Domain

This strategy involves making money by renting out a parked domain (by "parked" means not in use) you bought or registered to a third party who is interested in using it as a backdoor or redirecting website. Parked domains can also be used by a client to contain advertisements.

Why is an empty website worth something?

First, it is a free billboard that any client can use however wanted. Second, the domain name is probably essential to somebody's marketing campaign, like if it is more appropriate than their current domain name. That brings this discussion to the one crucial rule to make this strategy lucrative: you need to have a domain that other parties will want to have.

### 47. Podcasts/Audio Files

Not many people have the time to read entire books, so they often resort to audio files that they can listen to while driving, eating, or resting. Although text reader softwares are now available to convert eBooks to audio files, many people still prefer to hear natural voices like they are tuning in to a webinar or live seminar. You can bank on that if you have a good topic to discuss that you can turn into a series.

### 48. Plug-in Sales

As the sales of smartphone applications and PC games grow bigger, so does the plug-in market. The need for website customization has been growing in demand, and because a lot of owners do not have the resources to hire graphic specialists and programmers, they just take advantage of the available programming capabilities and maximize it with the use of plug-ins. WordPress users in particular have a huge demand for it.

You might hit the sweet spot with this market if you have an extensive background in programming and software development.

## 49. App Development

The top app developers make five digits a month (or even more!) just by creating and selling applications meant for smartphones and computers. Play Store's huge virtual shelves are a clear testament to that. You can design games, office applications, or even anything silly but interesting. Because this is not a high-end market, entry-level apps are very much welcome. In fact, the app development niche has been considered as the new go-to by students trying to make a living.

If you are not into technicalities, you can outsource the development and just take charge on the marketing side afterwards.

## 50. eBook Publishing

Under Amazon's Kindle Publishing Program, you can earn up to 70% of the entire sales if the purchase comes from one of the listed countries, such as US, UK, Canada, India, Japan, Germany, and others minus the transmission fee for every download. If you do not want any more deduction, you can opt for their 35% royalty program. For something that you have just written in a couple of days, you can earn limitlessly, which makes it one of the best passive income strategies there is.

Self-publication is easy, depending on the publishing program you want to try. Amazon publishers can have their works selling in as fast as 24 to 48 hours, while Barnes and Noble can have you listed in a couple of days. If you want to take all the earnings, you can sell it directly on your blog (although the marketing part will be a little tougher).

# Conclusion

Thank you again for purchasing this book on making money online!

I am extremely excited to pass this information along to you, and I am so happy that you now have read and can hopefully implement these strategies going forward.

I hope this book was able to help you understand the different ways to make money online and how to start doing them.

The next step is to get started using this information and to hopefully live a wealthier life free of financial worries!

Please don't be someone who just reads this information and doesn't apply it. The strategies in this book will only benefit you if you use them!

If you know of anyone else that could benefit from the information presented here please inform them of this book.

Finally, if you enjoyed this book and feel it has added value to your life in any way, please take the time to share your thoughts and post a review on Amazon. It'd be greatly appreciated!

Thank you and good luck!

# Preview Of:

# Hot Small Business Ideas!

*25 Smokin' Hot Start Up Business Ideas To Spark Your Entrepreneurship Creativity And Have You In Business Fast!*

# Introduction

I want to thank you and congratulate you for purchasing the book, *"Hot Small Business Ideas!: 25 Smokin' Hot Start Up Business Ideas To Spark Your Entrepreneurship Creativity And Have You In Business Fast!"*.

This book contains 25 proven small business ideas to find the right niche for you to become successful.

Congratulations on making the first step towards a better life for yourself and your loved ones. Creating a business is the financially smartest thing you can do in today's often volatile job market. As more and more folks get laid off in the rapidly changing economy we live in, more and more people are looking for a more stable source of income in which they have better control of.

I could go on and on about the benefits of owning and operating your own business, but I won't because that's not why you are here. You already know you want to own your own business and make your own decisions, you just need to know where to channel your drive and hard work. In this book you will find 25 of the Hottest Small Business Ideas for today!

One thing I have learned over the years of being an entrepreneur is that if you don't have passion for the business you are in - then you most likely will not make it. I'm here to fuel that passion by giving you some great ideas you can really sink your teeth into.

Thanks again for purchasing this book, I hope you enjoy it!

# Chapter 1 - Starting Your Own Online Business

Nobody gets rich by remaining an employee forever. You need to take greater risks, invest and be your own boss to earn more and provide a much better life for yourself and your family. That is practically how your bosses does it.

There is no better time to start a small business than now. Marketing has never been easier, thanks to the multitude of channels, tools and online facilities that help you have success in marketing without spending a dime. The awareness in business management is also higher, so you will have more time and opportunities to thrive in your chosen industry and make a name for yourself.

Starting your own business is not just about the extra income; it is about the extra time for yourself and your family, and all the comfortable and luxurious perks that come with it. Starting your own smoking hot business is your ultimate ticket to better living, having all resources to buy whatever you want and plan ahead without having to consider vacation/leave credits, office schedules and unrelenting superiors.

Being your own boss is a life-changing decision that can steer your whole life – upwards if you have the dedication and willingness to learn and develop your craft, or downwards if you cannot commit to your decision.

For a starter, you will be introduced to the hottest online businesses you can possibly start.

*1. Amazon Affiliate*

Affiliate programs are smoking hot; double that for Amazon. This is the new version of product consignment, only done online. You will need to do the marketing, promotions and reviews preferably in the form of blogging to get more customers for Amazon's listed products. This is a fulltime online business with unlimited earning opportunities.

*Pros:*

- *Famous* – Amazon is the top online shopping site all around the world. The name sells in itself. The program is reliable and has been around for more than a decade now. It is definitely the most trusted affiliate program today.

- *Flexible time* – All the marketing efforts and website setups are all in your good time. You can keep earning while sleeping, so management is not stressful.

- *Low-cost* – Your only expense is the domain and server, although there are free providers you can choose from.

*Cons:*

- *Might take time to pick up* – Gaining huge online traffic and website contents may take time, perhaps months before you can actually earn. The good thing is that when it picks up, there is no stopping it.

- *Requires intense internet marketing know-how* – Millions of people all around the world do marketing online. If you want to standout, you need to master the techniques and learn continuously.

2. Niche Blogging

Blogging doesn't run out of steam, and it continues to be the new newspaper, magazine, paperback, diary and variety show. According to Yahoo, the blogging industry recorded its highest revenue in 2013, and there is no sign of backing down anytime soon. Average niche bloggers earn anywhere from $1,000 to $15,000 a month, the latter implying the full-timers.

*Pros:*

- *Unlimited source of income* – You can earn from ad vendors, paid advertising, PPC, paid publicity and promotions, affiliate programs and dozens more of innovative online opportunities.

- *Easy to set up* – You only need to have flair in writing – informing and entertaining at the same time. Setting up your blog is easy and in fact, you can have it for free. Just pick a topic and niche market you want to tap, and be the best in it.

*Cons:*

- *Traffic problems* – Online traffic can be a big problem if you will only focus on the actual blogging part. Remember that this is a business; thus, it involves intense marketing and customer relations.

- *Requires patience* – You can't write and have thousands of readers right away. Even the most successful bloggers today needed to build their fan-base over time.

## 3. SEO Firm

SEO (search engine optimization) is the life of websites, both non-profit and commercial. SEO dictates the competition. It doesn't run out of market. Your business' goal here is to get clients on top of search engines and get them the traffic and conversion that they are targeting. If you have advance knowledge in web and graphic designing, SEO writing, SEM (search engine marketing) and internet marketing strategies, you are ready to get some clients and build websites for them. A team of five specialists is already enough to handle a pool of business websites.

*Pros:*

- *Easy to set up* – What you do when you make your own website or blog is the same thing you will do for your clients. You might just need support staff for the other technical aspects and to finish projects on deadlines.

- *Low-cost* – Most likely, you already have a usable computer. You only need to buy different software (you can get them for free if you are adept in online sourcing) and additional computers – perhaps rent a server.

- *Easy to market* – Your body of work speaks for itself. The market is unlimited, and your efficiency in the job will dictate how far you can get in the industry.

*Cons:*

- *Tough competition* – At the end of the day, your client's online success (in terms of traffic generation, search engine ranking, etc.) will gauge your reputation. There is only one page to aim at but, there are thousands of websites competing. The competition is not only between you and other SEO firms. You need to remember that your client's stand in the competition is also your responsibility.

## 4. Graphic Designing

You can launch this business as a part of SEO services for company websites and professional bloggers. However, a graphic designing company can also stand alone as it really was before SEO became the buzz. If you are adept in designing, working on your own shouldn't be a problem at all.

You can cater to bloggers and social media addicts who want to take their accounts to another level (many Facebook-ers and Youtube-ers hire graphic and video designers and editors to professionalize their accounts). You can also cater to special occasions, such as weddings, birthday parties, launchings, etc.

*Pros:*

- *Wide, unlimited market* – Graphic designing services have been here even before they were integrated with SEO. Specifically, those who hire graphic

- designers belong to small-scale businesses and private individuals. Your own talent will be your own setback.

- *Low startup cost* – You need a piece of computer, internet connection, printer and a whole lot of creative ingenuity. Depending on the volume of your clientele, you can expand in resources as you expand in operation.

*Cons:*

- *Professionally limiting* – Many experts believe that graphic designing should just be the beginning of a more expansive business because this alone is very limiting, professional at least. There's not exactly a next level, unless you include other services and provide tangible products as well, such as selling your own souvenir items or expanding to other SEO services as well.

## 5. eBook Self-Publication

Book and eBook writing are both professions, but self-publication of eBooks is a business. It involves end-to-end processes, from the writing to editing, cover designing to online publication, and marketing to selling. Many bloggers have already shifted to fulltime eBook self-publication as the potential income is higher.

Amazon and Barnes and Noble are the two top online destinations when it comes to eBook publication. You will likely receive just a percentage of the eBook price, but the accumulated earnings are enough to top your monthly income from a fulltime office job. Selling through your own website is also a lucrative idea, but only if you attract huge online traffic and has already set yourself as one of the leaders in your niche industry.

*Pros:*

- *Unlimited earning potential* – As of 2012, eBook sales have already surpassed hardcover sales, but only next to paperback sales. In the next five to 10 years, it is expected that online publication will be the most marketable form of publication.

- *A potential launch pad to stardom* – This business is not only about the money – millions of money. It is also about legacy, name and popularity.

- *Easy to execute* – Writing shouldn't be a problem. Most of your efforts will go to the cover design and marketing strategies.

*Cons:*

- *Needs decent online presence* – If you will market your own eBooks, you need to have an existing market-base. Otherwise, starting from scratch will take time to convert into sales.

- *Possible failure* – The failure in the self-publication industry is really high. Many eBook writers don't even crack the 200-sales threshold. If you think your writing skills and creativity are not enough to make a name for yourself, better choose another business.

## 6. eBay Trading

eBay is the best channel to start a trading business because all types of products are allowed, both new and used. The site is famous for its cheap finds, so pulling a chunk of the market should not be a problem.

You can source out your products from wholesalers, abroad, garage sales, or you can restore old items to make them new.

*Pros:*

- *High traffic volume* – Six out of 10 internet users have bought an item from eBay. That is how often eBay makes a sales, which means that market is far from being saturated anytime soon.

- *Easy to set up* – When you already have products to sell, you only need a camera, computer and basic knowledge in setting up an eBay account. You can do your own internet marketing, but eBay is already an established shopping destination. Customers go to the site without prodding.

- *Low startup cost* – Depending on your items, your capital can be as low as a couple of hundreds of dollars. It doesn't matter if you sell second-hand items.

*Cons:*

- *Difficulty with logistics* – This shouldn't really be a problem because dealing with forwarding and logistic company, both local and international, is now simpler. Nonetheless, you need to take care of it as well, which means extra work.

*7. Content Creating*

Others call it SEO and technical writing, but content writing is more than just a single component of a fulltime SEO firm. Content writing is less focused on internet marketing stuff – just plain quality content. In the 90s, content writing referred to the outsourced company magazine contents, that included internal newsletters, free magazine giveaways (as a part of store promos) and local ads.

Today, content writing primarily refers to website and blog writing, mostly of private organizations that use their websites not as primary marketing channels but as information centers (which is true for most consumer products that do not really sell online).

*Pros:*

- *High expected revenue* – Yahoo considers content writing as one of the biggest profession for the next 50 years, especially now that everything is shifting to online publication. The revenue and market are likely to expand without stopping.

- *Simple organizational structure* – A small content writing business doesn't even need to have an office. Most similar companies pool writers online and have them work in virtual offices. You can even do it by yourself if you will take one client at a time.

*Cons:*

- *Quality concerns* – For a bigger clientele, quality control might be a problem, especially when you do not have in-house editors to help you do quality control, proofreading and copyediting.

*8. Server Management*

Buying a dedicated server is not something that many small businesses can afford or are even willing to invest in. Server management companies then buy a server space and have it leased out to small companies. You can also have your own server and have it rented as shared server to several clients.

In addition, you must offer support and website management services.

*Pros:*

- *Huge ROI* – Leasing out a server alone may not incur impressive income, but because of the additional services, you can place a huge premium on top.

- *Huge market-base* – This is a very timely business, so relevant in today's business environment that will not run out of prospective clients in the next few years.

*Cons:*

- *Requires technical expertise* – Basic knowledge in server management is not enough. You need to have advance skills to make sure that your services are on top.

- *Limited clients* – The size of your clientele will depend on the size of your server.

# Thanks for Previewing My Exciting Book Entitled:

# "Hot Small Business Ideas! 25 Smokin' Hot Start Up Business Ideas To Spark Your Entrepreneurship Creativity And Have You In Business Fast!"

To purchase this book, simply go to the Amazon Kindle store and simply search:

"SMALL BUSINESS IDEAS"

Then just scroll down until you see my book. You will know it is mine because you will see my name "James Harper" underneath the title.

Alternatively, you can visit my author page on Amazon to see this book and other work I have done. Thanks so much, and please don't forget your free bonuses

**DON'T LEAVE YET! - CHECK OUT YOUR FREE BONUSES BELOW!**

**Free Bonus Offer 1: Get Free Access To The [OperationAwesomeLife.com](OperationAwesomeLife.com) VIP Newsletter!**

**Free Bonus Offer 2: Get A Free Download Of My Friends Amazing Book "Passive Income" First Chapter!**

**Free Bonus Offer 3: Get A Free Email Series On Making Money Online When You Join Newsletter!**

## GET ALL 3 FREE

Once you enter your email address you will immediately get free access to this awesome **VIP NEWSLETTER**!

For a limited time, if you join for free right now, you will also get free access to the first chapter of the awesome book **"PASSIVE INCOME"**!

And, last but definitely not least, if you join the newsletter right now, you also will get a free 10 part email series on **10 SUCCESS SECRETS OF MAKING MONEY ONLINE!**

To claim all 3 of your FREE BONUSES just click below!

Just Go Here for all 3 VIP bonuses!

## OperationAwesomeLife.com

CPSIA information can be obtained
at www.ICGtesting.com
Printed in the USA
LVHW081546130219
607421LV00031B/1095/P